Don't Blame Fred
Build Blame-Free Processes

Process Improvement Stories

From Successful Projects

Bill Flury

Copyright© 2018 -- Bill Flury

All rights reserved

ISBN-13: 978-1979178846

ISBN-10: 1979178844

ACKNOWLEDGEMENTS

Thanks to all my friends and colleagues who have encouraged and enabled me to share stories from the many, successful projects on which I have been privileged to work. Thanks to Chris Fristad for his encouragement to produce this compilation of stories and his constructive comments through the years as I have been writing them.

Special thanks to Vicki Wrona for inviting me into her blog at ForwardMomentum.net and for publishing the initial versions of these stories. Vicki's top-notch editorial team: Ray Robinson, Cheri Milford, and Natasha Egan have added graphics and arranged and presented the stories very well in the blog.

Diana Fraser provided essential design and editing advice. The illustrations were produced with the aid of software applications by Wordle.com and Caricature Software.

Special thanks to Mary Flury who has patiently supported me in so many ways throughout our many years together and especially through the gestation of this product.

Stories stimulate curiosity. People will seldom read procedure manuals, but most will eagerly devour short stories, even off the job.

Stories are memorable. The messages stemming from a particular experience tend to stick and can be easily recalled.

Edward Hoffman
Project Management Success Stories
John Wiley & Sons, 2000

Foreword

Learning to Succeed

Learning how to achieve success as a project manager can be difficult. Many experts and organizations have published detailed lists of standard practices and procedures one should follow to help ensure success. However, every project is unique, and the standard processes need to be adapted to fit real-life situations as they unfold.

Learning Through Stories

In 1998, Alexander Laufer and Edward Hoffman conceived a new way to help current and future project managers learn how to become successful. They sought out successful project managers and asked them to tell stories about their projects. They collected these and published them in a book titled *"Project Management Success Stories."* Their book contains 70 stories by 38 different project managers.

Those stories bring to life the many ways that the theoretical principles from the procedure manuals can be effectively and successfully applied. The situations described in the stories are real. The projects from which those stories come have all been successfully accomplished, not by theoretical people in the assumed situations in the procedure manuals, but by real people in real-life situations,

The Hoffman book has been very well received and is still a top seller. The stories are short, usually just a few pages. Readers who are currently working as project managers frequently find stories that relate situations like their own. Some read the stories to learn about situations they may face in the future.

Using the Stories

In their book, Laufer and Hoffman relate the story of one project manager who used it by reading one story each evening before he went to bed. About that, he said: *"Each morning when I got up I could not stop thinking about the previous night's story. I kept thinking about it as if it was an ongoing movie. Whenever I finished a story I added another milestone on my road to success."*

That reader provided evidence that each story offers one or more special insights that you can weave into your understanding of how to make projects successful in real-life situations.

This Book

In this book, you will find stories drawn from the author's experience in successfully managing 85 challenging and widely varied projects. The stories all relate to situations that required thoughtful application of the standard practices described in the several different process improvement and project management handbooks on his bookshelf.

ForwardMomentum.net

Versions of these stories were published over the past three years in an exceptional on-line blog published by Forward Momentum, LLC. Each month, that blog presents a collection of new stories by several of their more than thirty contributors on a variety of topics related to their successful projects and process improvement activities. The Forward Momentum archive contains more than 365 stories from the past three years, enough to provide bed-time reading for a whole year.

A Good Story

A good story is often the best way to convey meaningful knowledge.

L. T. Davenport
Developing Organizational Memory Through Learning
Organizational Learning, Autumn 1998

Onward to the Stories

But, first, read about how "The Rule of Fred" makes it too easy when things go wrong to blame people rather than the process and why that is so unfair.

CONTENTS

FOREWORD	v
Introduction	1
What's the Matter with Fred?	5
Don't Blame Sarah Either	11
More Stories	17
See How We Stopped Being Late	21
Work and Fun: Partners for Success	27
We Held a Best Practices Meeting and Nobody Came	33
Motivating Process Improvement	37
Where There's a Wall, There's a Way!	47
Tangible Benefits of a Well-Defined Process	53
The Project Manager's Mirror	59
Repealing the Rule of Fred	63
Do It Yourself Process Development Exercise	67

The Rule of Fred

When things go poorly, a team will easily break up and everyone will point fingers. Who's to blame?

"The team is very disappointed Fred at your failure!"

If a team doesn't have a Fred, they should get one, in case there's a failure! It's much easier to blame Fred than to take responsibility as a team.

When Fred succeeds, the team succeeds and can cheer its success, as a team. But when Fred fails, the team can scorn him and boo him and tell him, to work harder, or smarter or something.

"If only Fred had been a team player, we would have succeeded!"

This is the Rule of Fred.

Jason Giecek

Introduction

The Rule of Fred in Action

Something has gone wrong on your team's project. Your schedule has started to slip, the new product you are all working on is not working right, and the project is starting to go over budget or --- something else. Whatever it is, it is not good. That's when the **Rule of Fred** kicks in.

It must be somebody's fault that things are going wrong. Who might that be? ---"Fingers start to point to Fred!"

>*"Fred is taking too much time to complete his tasks."*

>*"Fred is overrunning his budget."*

>*"Fred is using the wrong materials."*

>*"Fred forgot to include the critical part."*

>*... and so on.*

It may very well be true that Fred did one of those things that triggered the problem, but why?

About Fred

Fred is a team member, just like you. He is a hard-working, conscientious member of the team. He comes to work every day wanting to do a good job. He pays close attention to his work and when he's asked to do something, he follows directions and tries hard not to screw up.

Fred has always done exactly what he has been tasked to do. He has applied himself to his assigned tasks and has efficiently used the time and materials he has been authorized to use. Somehow, something Fred has done has led to the current problem. If you look carefully, you will find that you should blame the process. You should not blame Fred. You and your team should be examining your processes to find what caused Fred to do what he did.

What Caused Fred to Do That?

To get a better understanding of what has happened, you should ask a few questions:

- Was it clear what Fred was tasked to do?
- Did Fred do what was called for in that process and, if not:
    - Was he given enough time and the right tools and materials to do what he was tasked to do?
    - Was he properly trained to do what he was asked to do?
- Did Fred get the correct inputs he needed for his part of the work when he needed them?
- Was there something in the process that led Fred to do something that caused the problem?

Finding the answers to those questions will reveal that the real fault lies somewhere in the team's project management and work processes. Something in those processes caused Fred to do (or not do) whatever triggered the problem.

It's the Processes

There are some fortunate souls who work where the work processes are well-defined and maintained and work always goes smoothly. However, there are still many places where problems like those mentioned above continue to occur frequently and the teams just continue to blame someone. They never stop and look for the real cause of the problems. So, the local "Freds" or "Fredas" keep getting blamed, the faulty processes remain unchanged, and the problems continue. That's no fun for anyone.

Avoid Blaming – Start Fixing

In this book you will see stories about real-life situations in which Fred and many other hard-working, sincere people appear to have problems and, like Fred, should not be blamed. In these stories, when there is a problem, the fault is in the project management or work process – *it's always the process* -- and the process should rightly be blamed for the problems – and fixed.

These Examples

The stories come from projects that have become consistently successful by focusing on their project management and work processes. So, as you read the stories, think of how they relate to your work, the problems you run into, and the way you want to deal with them.

And remember --

Don't Blame Fred

Fix the Process

===

Several years ago I was on a project team with Fred. His situation was the inspiration for the book. ------------------------------------->>>>>>>

===

What's the Problem with Fred?

About Fred

Fred is one member of a small group of technical experts who design and build specialized products that include both hardware and software. Fred is a "super coder," that's a very special kind of computer programmer.

The computer code that Fred writes is a key part of most of the active projects in his workgroup. He comes to work early and leaves late most days and his output is always good.

If you ask Fred to do something he will always agree to take it on and he will add it to his list. Fred usually has at least 8 or 9 things on his personal "To Do" list on his computer. Fred's list is in order by "Due Date." A lot of the dates are very close, and they are all marked "Urgent." Every morning Fred comes in and looks at his "To Do" list on his computer and gets to work on the next item on the list. Fred works on the items as fast as he can and turns out a huge amount of work.

Tasking Fred

New requirements come in daily from customers. Some of those are new requirements for new products and others are for modifications of requirements for products already in progress. The team usually has about 15 such projects going at any one time. It is vital for these products to be available at the time they are scheduled to be delivered.

A project leader who needs something from Fred for his project figures out what it was he needs and then discusses it with Fred. Fred, as always, says "I can do that." Then, Fred enters the task on his To Do list. Project leaders always consider the tasks in their projects as the most important, and the most urgent. That's the same way mothers think of their children. There is an old saying that has been translated into many languages. One of the more colorful versions is: "Every monkey in the eyes of his mother is a gazelle." Every project leader tells Fred that his task (his monkey) is the most critical. So, each task joins Fred's queue of baby gazelles on his To Do list.

As far as Fred knows, all the tasks are ***"urgent, important, needed as soon as possible, etc.."*** so, he works on them as fast as he can.

Is Fred The Problem?

Lately, the group had been missing deadlines and the leaders whose projects were late were saying that they were being held up by Fred's work. The number of Fred's missed deadlines was serious, and the group decided to try to fix it. There was no viable way open to refuse any of the incoming requirements. They could not reduce the group's workload. So, they had to figure out how to get the kinds of things Fred did when they needed them to complete their projects on schedule.

Fred was very productive. Fred was already working a lot of overtime and they did not want to work him any harder. They thought about getting more Freds. However, Fred's skills were truly unique so that option was out. All the things Fred was tasked to do he could, eventually, get done. He could turn out as much product as needed every day. The problem was that some of the things he was doing really weren't needed right away and others, farther down his list, were needed yesterday.

There was an overall schedule posted and maintained for all the projects. Each project lead managed his own project's schedule and pressed to get the work done on time to meet the current schedule. However, as they discovered, there was no schedule for the one critical item that affected almost every project – the various tasks they had asked Fred to accomplish.

Visibility to the Rescue

Each of the project leads was assuming that Fred was doing what they had asked him to do. None of them had any idea of what other work was on Fred's To Do list. So, we asked Fred to print out his To Do list. Here is a picture of what it looked like:

Fred's Sked		Today = 2 September
TASKS	Estimated Hours	Due Date
New Module – Project C	24	3-Sep
Fix Security – Project A	28	6-Sep
Adjust parameters – Project B	22	10-Sep
New Module – Project X	22	4-Sep
New Module – Project Y	30	8-Sep
Change Exit Report – Project C	18	12-Sep
Delete Useless Code – Project B	12	20-Sep
New Module – Project - S	14	16-Sep

Fred's list on the computer was in order by when he was asked to do the task. To get a different look, we asked him to sort it by due date with the nearest dates at the top. That gave us a much different picture. **(See next Page)**

Now All Could See

Now, for the first time, we could all see what tasks Fred was working on to try to meet the deadlines – and so could Fred. We could clearly see that there were not enough hours in Fred's work week (and overtime) to do all the work that had been requested to be completed for each week.

It now was very clear that Fred was way overbooked. He had 74 hours of work due this week and 52 hours that the project leads wanted to have done by the end of next week. Something had to give. Now the three project leaders had to talk and agree to adjust their deadlines.

Fred's Sked		Today = 2 September
TASKS	Estimated Hours	Due Date
New Module – Project C	24	3-Sep
New Module – Project X	22	4-Sep
Fix Security – Project A	28	6-Sep
This Week Total	**74**	
New Module – Project Y	30	8-Sep
Adjust parameters – Project B	22	10-Sep
Next Week Total	**52**	
Change Exit Report – Project C	18	12-Sep
New Module – Project - S	14	16-Sep
Delete Useless Code – Project B	12	20-Sep
Coming Up	**44**	

This was an eye-opener for the project leads and for Fred. Fred already knew he was taking on too much, but he didn't think it was his place to tell a project lead that he had to change his schedule. His job was to just get all the work done as fast as he could.

Aha! – The Problem Isn't Fred

We concluded that the problem wasn't Fred. The problem was that the project leads had not been looking at Fred's existing commitments before tasking him to do new work. The problem was theirs, not Fred's.

Fred and the project leads needed to set up a simple process to keep Fred's schedule visible and to support the orderly negotiations of deadlines. They found that the "Fred's Sked" spreadsheet worked well. Now Fred keeps the current version of that posted on the outside wall of his cubicle. The project leads consult it regularly as they work on their project schedules to integrate Fred's tasks with all their other tasks.

The Real Problem

The problem was a flaw in the group's process for assigning work. No one in the group could see the overload on Fred's schedule. Printing out and posting the current version of the Fred Sked on the portal to Fred's cubicle exposed the problem and provided a mechanism for the Project Leaders to see potential scheduling problems and resolve them before they became a problem. When they could see the flaw in the process they could fix it.

Benefits of the Improved Process

Now Fred never has to struggle to get 70 or 80+ hours of work done in a week. He still usually works more than 40 hours a week, but he is happier now because the negotiated deadlines are much more reasonable, and he is meeting them.

===

Next, you will get to meet Sarah. She was unfairly being blamed for some problems and asked for help.

===

Don't Blame Sarah, Either

Let's move on to Sarah's tale. She is a publications coordinator. She works with engineers and graphics artists. She's been getting blamed by both groups for a lot of mix-ups in the graphics and she can't see why. Wait till you see the problem she had and how she resolved it.

You may have a problem like hers and could do what she did to solve it.

Don't Blame Sarah Either

Sarah Has a Problem

Sarah was having a bad day, one of many in the past few weeks. Things just weren't working as she expected them to. She was doing what she had been doing all along but, for some reason, some things were not going right. She couldn't see what was happening. She asked me if there was some way I could help her see what was causing the problems.

Sarah worked in a high-tech organization that was staffed by a lot of engineers and programmers. They did analyses, conducted studies, and developed designs and produced reports about those things for their clients. Sarah's job was to take the draft reports produced by the staff, get them paired with the appropriate graphics, get them to conform to the company formatting standards, and prepare them for final printing and delivery.

At our first meeting, I asked Sarah to show me in detail what she did, so we could walk through the process and discuss it. Sarah gave me a quick overview of what she did. She mentioned that in the last few weeks some of the engineers had told her that they were upset about the graphics being produced for their reports. They felt that charts being produced by the graphics staff were not accurately reflecting the story in the data. On the other hand, the graphics staff were complaining that the engineers weren't providing enough background information about the data. Sarah said that she was getting caught in the middle of the arguments as she tried to get everything pulled together for publication.

It's All in My Head

It sounded like there was some flaw in the process that was causing these problems and we should try to find that flaw and fix it. So, I asked Sarah, "Do you have a written description of what you do?" Sarah said, "No." "Do you have notes that you took when you were being shown or told what to do?" Sarah said, "No." "Do you have a checklist or a set of instructions, or a manual that you follow? Sarah said, "No." She finally said, "It's just all in my head."

We agreed that just having it all in her head was not very good. We couldn't use that to find and fix any flaws in the process. There were several problems. First, what she was seeing in the head was obviously not clear enough to enable her to see what was causing her frequent problems. Second, we discussed the fact that what she was seeing in her head, her "Mind's Eye" so-to-speak, was an imperfect picture. She might be missing some of the details or remembering some things wrong. Finally, I told her I had to be able to see it also, so we could work together to get what was causing her problems.

Seeing What's in Sarah's Head

As we started, I told her about something said by Bernard DeVoto, a great editor: *"The best thing about writing something down is that then you can change it."*

Then, I said, "Trying to work with something you can't see (because it's not written down) is like trying to make a suit of clothes for a ghost. It won't work. So, we will have to work together to get it written down. Then we can find out what's not working and change it. So, go ahead and "wing it" – explain to me, from memory, what you do, and we'll record it on the chalkboard."

Sarah started talking and I started drawing what she said as a process flow chart on the chalkboard. In the first pass, Sarah talked though everything she was doing. I kept drawing and writing notes as she talked. When Sarah got to the end, we both took a short break and then came back to look at the result.

Then, we walked through the flow chart again. Sarah saw things she had missed and some things that had not been correctly recorded. We fixed the chart so it accurately represented what Sarah was doing.

Then, I asked a Sarah a few questions.

- Are there some things you do without thinking?
- Are there some things you only do in certain circumstances?
- Do you have any checklists, "Post-Its" or other kinds of notes or reminders about any parts of this process?
- Are there any things in this picture that you think you do but, really, never do?

Those triggered Sarah's memory and we made a few additions and changes to the picture. Then, we wrote "SAVE" on the chalkboard and left for the night.

The Next Day

The next day we asked two of the engineers who were frequent authors to come and walk through the chart with us. They clarified a few points and changed one task that required checking for documentation standards. That involved two steps instead of the one shown. Later in the day we did the same with two of the graphics staff members and had similar results.

Then We Began to See

The following day, we walked through the chart together. One thing became very clear. All the communication between the authors and the graphics people went through Sarah. There were no places in the flow chart where those two groups ever talked directly with each other. All the products from each group passed Sarah on the way to the other. Likewise, and here was a key point, all the complaints and problems also went through Sarah and she, as a coordinator did not have authority to provide technical direction to either group.

Sarah thought about that for a moment and then commented. She said that it seemed unfair that she was being caught up in the arguments between the two groups. She said, "I think I see the problem. The problems we are having are their problems, not mine, and I should not be in the middle."

She looked back at the chart and said, "You know, if we added a task for the authors and the graphics people to get together while their documents are being drafted …"

The Lessons for all Involved

Creating the flow chart was, literally, an eye-opener for Sarah. As she was drawing the chart she was reminded of things that she and her co-workers did in the process that they did without thinking. She also saw gaps in the process where there were things she did not know or had forgotten. When she was done, for the first time, Sarah could clearly see how the whole process worked and how she and the others fit into it. She got a more complete understanding of what she needed to do to make the process work better. What she could see, she understood. Sarah needed help to recall, describe, and define the details of her process and the relationships among the players.

When the things she was doing were only "in her head" they were floating about and were invisible to her and not really useful. Some details had been forgotten and the sequencing of actions was not as clear as it was later when the picture was put up on the chalkboard. The problem was hiding in

the details and Sarah had to bring out the details, make them visible, and stabilize them so she could see and get what was going on.

Success

Once the process was written down and visible on the chalkboard, as Bernard DeVoto told us, she could change it, and she did. Now, the process works smoothly and there's no blaming Sarah.

===
Now, we will move onto more stories ------------------------------>>>>>>>
===

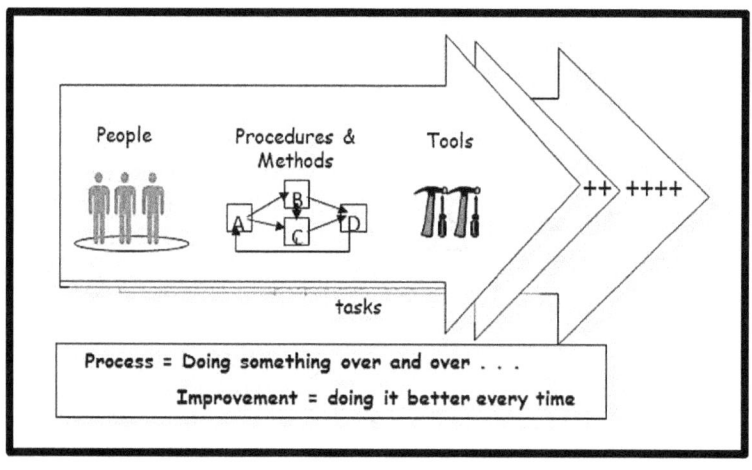

More Stories

Process Threats to Project Success

There's a lot at stake when your organization's processes don't work smoothly. If your processes don't perform well, your company won't do well. Clients may drop you because of late or shoddy work. Competitors may pull ahead of you. Potential clients may not even allow you to bid for work if you can't demonstrate consistent, reliable processes. So, if you fail to act to make your processes work well, you can end up with a mega process headache – no job!

Good Process – Key to Success

Observe successful project teams for a while and you will discover their secret. Over time, they have analyzed what has gone well and what has not on prior projects and developed a robust process that they use to tackle each new project that comes their way. They have addressed the fact that all projects are different and have developed a process that effectively deals with the variations.

Process Success Stories

This section presents seven stories drawn from the author's experience with project teams that had to discover ways to become successful. The stories illustrate the wide range of issues and attitudes those teams and their managers faced as they developed processes that would help them guarantee success.

See How We Stopped Being Late

This first story is about an advertising agency group that develops the specialized printed matter (e.g., fancy brochures, imprinted objects) that the client wants to be able to hand out at  their press conference on the day of a new product launch. When these materials are not ready on the day of the launch the client gets very upset. There is always a penalty for missing the date and contract cancellation is always possible. The story tells how they fixed their process so that they would never again miss a delivery date.

Work and Fun: Partners for Success

This story is about a team that was having a lot of **Un-Fun** at work. In fact, things were so bad, they decided to find out where all the Un-Fun was coming from so they could kill it. They did just that and got a pleasant surprise. In the process of killing off the Un-Fun, they started to have Fun. Now, all their projects succeed, and they can truly answer "Yes" when you ask them, "Are you having fun, yet?" You'll see how they succeeded in doing that.

We Held a Best Practices Meeting…

And Nobody Came?

This story and the next are both about groups that had no interest in process improvement. In fact, one group was actually hostile to the idea. In both stories the participants are "too busy" doing what they do to take time to figure out how to do it better. They continue to plod along, making the same errors again and again, working through unending crises and rarely succeeding.

Motivating Process Improvement

This story reveals some of the reasons that individuals and teams lack motivation to try to improve their work processes. It took a while for us to surface and understand their issues. Then, we worked with them to put them on a path to improving their processes. You might be surprised at some of the issues and the techniques used to address them.

Where There's a Wall, There's a Way!

This story is about a group that makes daily changes to a large database. They used to be plagued by errors in the delivered changes. They found that everyone was doing changes in a different way and that was causing the errors. See how they found a way to fix their process. Now, they don't make any errors.

Tangible Benefits of Having a Well-Defined Process

Teams that have developed successful process improvement programs have proved that process improvement activities are worth the effort required to implement them. This story is about the many tangible benefits that accrue. You can judge for yourself if getting those benefits might be worth some effort on your part.

Wish List
1. No useless work
2. No crises
3. Realistic schedule
4. No overloads
5. Work- Life Balance
6. Less overhead time
7. Carefree vacations

The Magic Mirror

The final story is a about a project manager who finds a Magic Mirror in a pawn shop. He takes it home, and they talk about how things are going on his project.

The mirror seems to know a lot about the project manager and feels free to offer some sound advice. Maybe you should think about getting a magic mirror?

===

Late Again

See How We Stopped Being Late

Another Missed Deadline

Advertising agencies work in close collaboration with their clients. They work together to develop the ideas for launching a new product and set a schedule for the launch. Then, the agency's back room goes to work to develop all the advertising materials the client wants to accompany the product launch.

This story is about an advertising agency group that develops the specialized printed matter (e.g., fancy brochures, imprinted objects) that the client wants to be able to hand out at their press conference on the day of the new product launch. When these materials are not ready on the day of the launch the client gets very upset. There is always a penalty for missing the date and contract cancellation is always possible.

So, the reason for this story -- **The group just missed a launch date for the third time this year.**

About the Group

The production group consists of four teams: Design, Ink, Paper, and Press. The members of each team are all very experienced and expert at what they do. Their products (when they are on time) are world-class.

The Design Team attends the client conferences. They provide designs for the products and specification for the printing and embossing. The Ink Team orders and mixes the inks required. Some of the inks needed to achieve special effects could be classed as exotic. The Paper Team reviews the product specifications from the designers and places orders for the paper. Again, some of the paper needed for special effects can be unusual and may require special ordering. The Press Team is the production team. They take all the inputs from the other teams and produce the final products. The typical time frame for all of this to occur is 90 days.

It sounds very straightforward, but it isn't. For the process to work well all the components have to work well together. The ink must be compatible with the paper or it will bleed or smear when being run through the presses. The paper needs to be compatible with the presses, so it won't jam or tear when it is being run. The designs are also sensitive to ink and paper issues. Some designs just won't "work" on certain types of papers.

The various team members were aware of all these possible incompatibilities and tried to avoid them. However, whenever they were late it was usually because they got a nasty "incompatibility surprise" somewhere along the way and one or more things would have to be done over with a different design, different materials or different press techniques.

What They Did About It

First, they all agreed that they had to fix their process, so they could do a better job of meeting deadlines. They asked for some help. We got a member from each team into the same room with a big whiteboard. Then, we wrote "Start" at the left edge of the board and "Deliver" on the right edge.

We asked each person to describe to the group everything they did between Start and Deliver. The facilitator worked at the chalkboard to capture what was being said in the form of a linear flow of tasks. As each team member described his teams' work the facilitator captured and drew that as a separate line. When they were done with their descriptions there were four separate flow charts, one for the work flow of each team.

As the next step, we asked each team member to estimate the amount of time it would normally take to perform each of the tasks on their line.

We made sure that their total did not exceed 90 days. Ideally, it would be much less.

What They Began to See

They discovered that there was no evidence of any coordination tasks in any of the task lines. Each unit was working to its own schedule, doing what it thought was required and not talking with the others about what was needed and when in order to meet the delivery date. The result was that delays were being caused by unforeseen mismatches of ink and paper, design and ink, or ink and press. It quickly became apparent to everyone that closer coordination was needed.

As they worked with the picture they concluded that there were three things they needed to do. First, they needed to add some early tasks to discuss and resolve potential incompatibility problems before they occurred. To accomplish this, they agreed on a way to coordinate their materials ordering and testing schedules that would substantially reduce the time needed for testing. Then they had to figure out how to line up all the tasks that depended on each other in a way that, when done in sequence, they would fit easily into the 90-day maximum schedule. Finally, they had to draw a new version of their picture to reflect their combined schedule.

Life After Headaches

The teams started to use the new chart as a process roadmap for their projects. They noticed improvements almost immediately. There were far fewer incompatibilities. Schedule slips became less frequent. Their performance is now consistent. Most important, they have not missed a deadline since the meeting.

This group has recognized that they can do even better. They have also recognized that their process picture might have to change from time-to-time as their clients and suppliers change.

Their process picture is posted on the wall in their hallway. The group now has a regular, once-a-month, Brown Bag lunch meeting where they walk through the process together and discuss potential improvements and agree on whether or not to change their picture. Anyone with an idea for how to make the process work better speaks up and, if they all agree that it would be an improvement, they change the picture.

In these gatherings they also re-affirm that they will be careful to follow the processes because that's the only way they can tell if it is really working.

The Lessons for all Involved

Each team had a very clear idea of what they did, but they had never shared that with the other teams. Getting the teams together and getting them to share and try to link their individual process flow charts exposed the situation that was causing the unwanted delays (e.g. the frequent incompatibilities among ink, paper, design). When the individual teams saw this for the first time, it was a great "Aha!" moment for them. The need to coordinate their special needs and schedules for each launch was obvious.

Late No More

When they all could see the whole process, they could see where the faults were, and they fixed them. Now, sometimes it's close but they never miss a deadline

==

Work & Fun

Work and Fun: Partners for Success

"Now Our Work is More Fun"

That's what our project teams say as they are reaping the benefits of their process improvement activities. We keep hearing this. They don't just say that things are going a lot better now than before. They do say that, but the  way they say it is that they are having more fun at work. Why do they choose to frame their answer that way instead of the usual business terms? What are they telling us?

Fifty Shades of Fun

In his book, **American Fun**, John Beckman discusses both Fun and Un-Fun related emotions. There's a long list and a wide range of Un-Fun activities. These include things that are so Un-Fun that they are sad, woeful, disagreeable, or unpleasant. Others that fit in this category are boring, tiring, or just plain unfunny. And, of course, Roget could probably suggest more.

In the Fun category we see things that are; pleasant, satisfying, entertaining and enjoyable. Fun seems to top out at boisterous — the unbridled "Jump in the air and yell WOO-HOO!" Fun.

- Thomas Edison's thousands of failed light bulb experiments were enjoyable for him even though they failed to find a working filament. Finding things that wouldn't work was the kind of thing he enjoyed. But the AHA! Moment when he found the one right element was pure, top level FUN.

- For a serious runner, running well in a marathon is satisfying, being among the front runners is enjoyable (better than just being satisfying) and winning is top-level FUN!

Beckham's taxonomy provides a basis for helping us figure out what these people are saying about the benefits of their process improvement activities when they say: "Now our work is more fun"

Living in an Un-Fun World

Our project teams consist of people who used to work in conditions one would call chaotic. They had processes that were poorly defined or non-existent – and almost never documented. Their regular workday was filled with unpleasant crises and disagreeable misunderstandings. They frequently had to apologize to our clients for woeful errors and faulty products and often had to work overtime to fix them. They would often fall behind schedules and, when they did, they could not get anyone to help because they didn't have procedures in place that described things  others could follow and pitch in to help. They felt trapped in chaos and their life at work was boring, tiring and a classic example of Un-Fun. Many of their co-sufferers left. Hiring their replacements was a big problem because everyone knew it was not a great place to work.

Some of the teams tried to get rid of the Un-Fun, (e.g., errors, schedule crises) by instituting rigid controls. Those helped achieve the basic business goals but were considered by the teams as just another form of Un-Fun and they did not like that approach. In their minds, having no Un-Fun was a prerequisite for continuing to work there.

Getting Rid of Un-Fun

The unhappiness of those who stayed led them to seek a prescription to rid them of all the Un-Fun in their lives. They found and settled on a process improvement program that outlined a set of simple things they could do to find and fix the things they were doing that were causing Un-Fun things to occur. It sounded demanding at first, so we retained some coaches to help them get started. They quickly found out that process improvement would be easier than they thought it was going to be.

The first thing they learned from their process improvement coaches was that they already had a process. The coaches asked them to do something they had never done before — draw a picture of their process showing what they were doing, exactly the way they were now doing it. Then, they could all look at it and figure out where and how the

Un-Fun things were coming from in the process. That first step, drawing a picture of their current process, let them all see many Un-Fun makers.

The first thing they noticed was that they all had somewhat different versions of what was supposed to be the common process. They spent a couple of weeks agreeing on a single version.

Then, they began to understand what was going on. Until then, they had been blaming each other for creating the Un-Fun problems. The blame-game stopped. Now, they realized that they all had been trying to make a bad process work. It was their process that was bad – not each other.

They agreed to make some changes to their process so the Un-Fun creating activities would no longer occur. Over the next several months they did this a few more times. What happened next?

The Death of Un-Fun

As the Un-Fun things started to go away, work began to flow more smoothly. With the process defined and documented, everyone knew who was supposed to do what and how things should be done. Work relationships among the team members smoothed out and the crises faded away and, along with that, unpaid overtime on nights and weekends also began to disappear. They began to have opportunities to spend evenings with their families and friends.

Those who had been embarrassed by errors before could see where the process they had been following had been causing the errors. They stopped feeling guilty about errors when they could see that they were being caused by faulty processes and not poor performance on their part. No longer feeling trapped in chaos, they were beginning to feel empowered to find and fix their most vexing problems.

They had arrived at what might be called neutral territory between Un-Fun and Fun. Things were not yet working completely smoothly but you could hear people say, "It's not as bad now as it used to be."

Are They Having Fun Yet?

For these groups, doing the simple basics of process improvement – defining and documenting their processes, following them, tracking results and feeding improvements back into the processes – has eliminated most of their Un-Fun.

Having less Un-Fun has also established a foundation for moving up the scale and making their work more satisfying and enjoyable. Here's what some of them have been doing.

- With the crisis pressure off, team members now have a chance to slip in a game of Foosball in the company break room from time to time. That's diverting and counts as a form of Fun.

- One of the teams has just celebrated completion of 100 days of error-free product deliveries. Their party was Fun.

- Unscheduled overtime pretty much disappeared and they got home earlier and could go to their kids' soccer games or to a show or concert. Those were Fun

- One of the groups used to have trouble winning proposals because of its poor performance record. Their win-rate has improved from 10% to 50% — well above average for their business. That's a very satisfying form of Fun.

- Another group is now consistently completing projects ahead of schedule and under budget. That's more than satisfying, that's really enjoyable – one more step up the Fun ladder.

Top Level Fun

Top level fun comes when you do something exceptional – something that is particularly difficult or unique or successfully done in the face of great odds. One of the top performing teams among the respondents has now been performing well for over a year. Nine months ago, they took over a project that was running late and was over budget. They re-worked the process and that helped them get ahead of schedule. At the meeting when they delivered the product to the customer a month early and on budget, they all jumped in the air and yelled WOO-HOO! Clearly, they were having more FUN.

What Are They Saying?

Today's technical workforce is very mobile and puts a high value on Fun. They have a low tolerance for Un-Fun and leave when they are having too much of it.

Those who tell us that they are having more Fun are those who are following the simple, cooperative approach to process improvement. They work together to draw and share a picture of what they do, share ideas on how to do it better, and do this continually. In addition to curing the business problems, the creativity involved in this process also makes it a form of Fun.

Their message for us is that their simple, self-directed process improvement activities have brought them more of what they value and that is their way to express it – more Fun. Their hidden message is that they would be gone if they were not having Fun.

We presently take and use metrics for cost, schedule and product quality. Perhaps we should consider one more – a metric for Fun.

===

Are YOU having Fun, yet?

*How do you eliminate **Un-Fun** from your work environment?*

===

We Held a Best Practices Meeting…
And Nobody Came?

First Meeting: A Great Idea

We were discussing how we could get started with the business of process improvement. Mickey said, "Hey! I've got a great idea! The Quality folks are always telling us that we should be on the lookout for better ways to do things. Let's hold a series of Best Practices workshops and see what ideas people bring us." We all thought it was a great idea.

We agreed that we should test the idea by each of us calling some key people in our respective centers and getting their reactions. What a surprise we got!!!!! The reaction to our calls was not anything like what we expected–but it did reveal a lot about our practices.

Reaction # 1 – "Gee, that sounds like a really great idea … but we don't have any Best Practices."

I'm not sure we even have anything that you could call a practice. Every job is different. Every customer is different. We have lots of thing we do, if you want to call those practices, but we just do what we think is best for each case.

Reaction # 2 – "How would you ever compare practices?

We don't really keep track from one project to the next on what we do. We rely on the memory of our key people. It's all in their heads and you can't compare what you can't see.

Reaction # 3 – "When you say Best Practices who are the practices supposed to be best for?"

So, who would we want to please with our Best Practices: (1) the customer; (2) our staff; (3) the supported and supporting systems with which our practices interface? For whom must we be best? That's a tough question.

Looking at it another way, it's hard to figure at what must we be best. Is the key (1) cost, (2) schedule, or (3) technical performance or (4) some combination.

Reaction # 4 – How could you ever convince everyone that one version of a practice is Best?

If we picked one practice and called it the Best, how would we ever be able to convince someone that that way is better than their way? Lots of people come up with ideas on how to do things better but nobody ever comes forward with any convincing data–just opinions–and they don't sell.

Second Meeting: A Better Idea

After hearing the reactions, we decided that it would be premature to try to hold the proposed workshops. We had to devise some way to start to attack the problems that had been raised. We decided to take some steps to start laying the foundation for identifying and evaluating the practices of our respective centers. Here's what we decided:

Problem # 1: — There are no standard practices–in fact there are not even any routine practices identified.

We will encourage everyone to start writing down or drawing a picture of the steps in their current practices. This is a necessary first step. It will provide the foundation for all measurements and comparisons.

Problem # 2: — There does not seem to be any basis for comparison among practices

We will ask everyone to line up all the variations of each practice and see how they are the same or different. (We think that they will find much more commonality than they expect.) We will encourage them to agree on some of the common items and start to use them in the same way on all projects. We will also start to work with them to see how they can begin to track variations in the outcomes.

Problem # 3: — We don't seem to know how to determine Best.

Instead of **Best**, we will start people thinking about the concept of **Better**. We will help them look for changes in their practices that might yield any improvements in cost, schedule or performance or might be better for the customer, the staff or associated organizations. We will help them test proposed changes and evaluate the outcomes.

Problem # 4 – How to convince people to start using practices identified as Better.

We need to make sure the practices are documented, consistently followed and the outcomes tallied. Then, we should be able to present convincing data on how different ways of performing the practices affect cost, schedule, and performance and how they affect the customer, the staff, and others.

Better Practices Workshops

We will start our hunt for Better Practices with a series of workshops with staff who are working on similar projects. Over the next few months, we plan to work with these groups to address the problems in the manner we have laid out. Our hope is that we can get on the path outlined in the poem attributed to Saint Jerome, who should be the patron saint of process improvement.

> *Good, Better, Best*
>
> *Never Let It Rest*
>
> *'Til the Good is Better*
>
> *and the Better, Best.*

===

===
How has your organization kept track of its Best Practices?
===

Motivating Process Improvement

Introduction

You would think that something that includes "improvement" in the title is good and should be in favor of it. However, it doesn't always play out that way. There are people who just don't see any need to improve what they are doing and lack any motivation to spend any time or effort doing it. Trying to force people with this attitude into a process improvement program almost always fails.

A frustrated manager of one of our production centers asked us to help him find a way to improve the performance of his teams. He had tried several ways to get them to do better work, but he had not been able to spark any interest in improvement. He asked us to talk with them to find out why they did not seem to care.

We interviewed them and discussed the results with the manager. Together, we came up with some ideas about how he might be able to motivate them to do better work.

Part 1: Lack of Motivation for Process Improvement

"We're Doing Fine."

Ask these workers about doing something to improve their processes and they say, "We're doing fine. Don't bother us with that stuff. Sure, we have mix-ups, make mistakes, and deliver our products late or with errors, but none of that is a problem for us or the company." So, why don't they care about that? Why doesn't all that give them headaches?

How can they feel that they are "fine" and don't need to improve the way they work? Read on.

"It's Not Really a Process."

These workers are software maintenance programmers. The type of work they do is similar to what auto mechanics do. All the jobs appear to be different and, in fact they are. However, the process that they follow in attacking each job and making the changes always includes the same kinds of tasks: analyze the problem; devise a change; write the "fix"; test the fix; deliver the change and adjust the documentation. It really is a process, but they can't see that. There is enough similarity in those jobs to make it possible to do them better, cheaper and faster – if one really wanted to. But, why? And, where would you start?

"We Get Paid for All the Hours We Work."

The workers involved in this process develop, test and deliver software changes to a government IT system. They work under the terms of a services contract. They, and their company, get paid for all the hours they work. That includes any time for extra work or rework before or after they deliver their products. It also includes payment for overtime when that is needed. In some contracts of this type there is premium pay for overtime and that is an incentive to create a need for it.

"There's No Personal Competition to Beat."

The workers have somewhat rare skills. They have had long-term experience with their client's IT system. They feel secure because it would be difficult for their client to replace them without a major disruption in their operations. The client cannot do the work with internal staff, so the client is quite tolerant of mistakes, errors and late deliveries.

"Why Work Faster, Better or Cheaper?"

There's never a deadline. The client's IT system has been in place for a long time and will continue for a long time to come. Changes are needed at a fairly steady rate and it is extremely rare to have a requirement to make a change by a certain date. When that does occur, other changes get deferred, so the workload stays steady. Improved response time has no value.

"Nobody Cares."

The work allows little opportunity for recognition. With no regular measurement of performance, management has no way to recognize and reward good performance. The workers get their psychic income from their peers. They know who the "best" is. That's enough for them.

"Why Bother?"

From the workers' standpoint, what's to improve? They work at a pace that suits them and get paid for every hour they work. They get paid for good work or bad. If they have to work overtime (for any reason) they get a premium. Their management is not concerned about the pace of their work because they can bill for every hour – and more is better. The client tolerates this because they have no other options.

They're "fine." But, are they, really? What if the company loses its permissive client and has to compete for work with one that is really concerned about cost, schedule and technical performance? On a personal level, what if the company can't compete and the workers need to find other jobs? What will they have to show for their past performance? Maybe they should care.

Now, let's listen to the Managers and hear why they are not interested.

"It's Not Required."

There are managers who stick closely to their work orders and contract terms. They have their work groups do only what is specified, nothing more. They will do process improvement only if it is required in their contract.

"We Just Sell Hours – Not Performance."

Few managers collect meaningful data on productivity or performance. With no meaningful data on either of these, it is hard to perceive how working differently (better) would make the company more competitive. Competition has to be on cost alone. No case can be made for productivity per hour. The company is just selling hours – good or bad, all hours are the same price. The only way they can improve on the hourly rate is to hire cheaper people and that's not process improvement.

"We're Doing Fine."

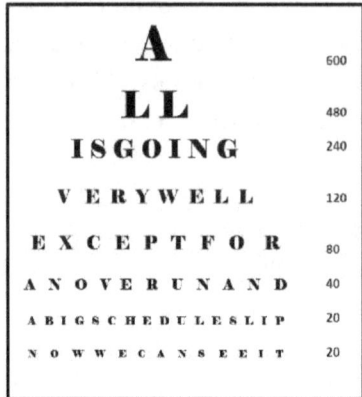

These managers are meeting their cost, schedule and performance goals and can prove that. In their minds, they are doing fine.

[Dirty little secret: They are not really doing fine. They are not counting the uncompensated overtime for rework and recovery from schedule slips and cost overruns. So, they really don't know how "UN-fine" they are.]

"It's Too Complicated and Costs Too Much."

Unfortunately, the jargon and complexity of formal process improvement programs are hard to understand and tend to confuse people. Process improvement consultants stress rigor and company managers often overreact to the advice. This leads them to misperceive and vastly overestimate the cost of putting a formal program into action. Already unaware and leery of the potential benefits, company managers approach the process improvement programs with great concern. Without being required to do such a program, few can be convinced of the value.

Part 2: Creating Motivation for Process Improvement

Effective process improvement programs have been shown to yield many benefits on both a personal and an organizational level. To motivate people to participate actively in a process improvement program you need to make sure everyone is aware of and fully comprehends the benefits to themselves and to their organization. However, the benefits are subtle and need to be revealed and explained to those who presently perceive no value. Without that, they will treat any proposed "improvement" program like bad tasting medicine. They will do their best to avoid the things they need to do to make it work.

Part 2: How to Change Attitudes Regarding Process Improvement

Getting a process improvement program into operation and working well is not easy. You must overcome some inertia – the feeling that "We're fine, why should we change what we're doing?"

Let's assume that you are the person who volunteered to accept this leadership challenge. To succeed you will need to turn the negative feelings of the work group into positive feelings for process improvement. Our approach for doing this can be summarized as Reveal, Appeal, and Deal. You should approach these in that order.

Reveal the Process

The biggest hurdle for you to overcome is the unjustified feeling that "what we are doing is not a process." You really do have a process. Your process is what you do. The problem is that, while everyone thinks they know what they do and how they interact with the others in their work group, there is no description of the process that everyone can see. Thus, your first task is to reveal the process so that all can see a complete picture of it.

You need to gather the folks who are doing similar types of work and get them to explain to each other their personal process for doing what they do. As they explain what they do you should all begin to see a common thread that runs through all their descriptions. You should work to develop a generic picture of the processes they are describing. Along with the generic description you should also note the variations and the reasons for them.

When you have all agreed on the generic description and the variations you should complete this part by drawing a chart of the process and posting it and the list of variations in a spot where all can readily see it. That initial chart will form the foundation for all further discussion of possible improvements.

Appeal to the Participants

Now that you have a chart of the process you can start tracking how the process works. You should start by taking some baseline measurements such as: (1) the shortest, longest, and average time to complete the process, or (2) the total amount of time per month spent on reworking things that had to be re-done.

Be careful to focus on the performance of the process, not on the work of the individuals performing the process. Process improvement is a team effort. If there is a problem in the process it is always a process problem, not an individual problem. *(Remember, "Don't blame Fred!)*

Once you have some initial process performance measurements you can appeal to the participants to see if they can come up with any ways to improve on them. When the process is inconsistently performed, work is no fun. Things get left undone or done poorly or late and people can get upset by the crises and the need to work late to fix problems or the other signs of process disarray. When it gets bad enough, some may want to make things work more smoothly – but may not know how a process improvement program can help. You must explain it to them and, even then, they may still think it's too hard and not worth the effort. So, you've got to be really convincing.

If you listen carefully to the people performing the process you may hear some ideas that will help everyone avoid some of the hassles and misunderstandings of how the work gets done. Bringing these to light for all to see should provide some incentive to try some process fixes (i.e., improvements) to make the process easier and more enjoyable.

Here is a testimonial from a guy who left a company where the processes were running smoothly and is now in a company where the process is best described as chaos, see the e-mail from David to his old boss. However, testimonials like that may not be enough. You may have to move on to the third component of this approach.

> **Subject**: Work
> **From**: davidz@xxx.com
> **To**: techldr@yyyy.com
> **Date**: Mon, 27 Mar 2017 15:58:00 -0600
>
> After working for a company that went from chaos to process, process has become an expectation. It's like getting a faster machine, and then changing employers and working with a slower machine.
> I'm back working in chaos, and a rare day goes by where I don't notice the difference.
>
> David

Deal with the Participants

This step brings together your organization's interests and your participant's interests. As noted before, an effective process improvement program provides a company with a strong competitive advantage and is valuable in marketing the services of the organization. It is worth something to the organization to set aside some marketing resources (money) to support development of a good process improvement program.

Losing a few bids because your company's costs were too high, or your references said that your work has been faulty or late makes a strong case for investing marketing resources in process improvement. However, even if your company has been competing well you have to remember the old Satchel Paige quote: "Never look back, they may be gaining on you." Don't forget, your competitors also know about process improvement and are practicing it. To stay competitive, you always must do better.

You Can Do It

So, consider setting up and funding a process improvement incentive program that will offer tangible rewards such as bonus money or free time to process participants when their process achieves measurable, marketable improvements. Such improvements could include documented error-free performance, predictable response times and lower costs per unit of output. There might also be some benefits in improved employee retention.

If you choose to take on the challenge, make sure that you reserve enough time and have the resources to do it. Keep it at the top of your priority list. Any slacking off in the effort will send a signal that you are not really serious about the program and you will lose whatever motivation you have been able to muster.

Keep It Simple

Keep what you do simple. Many companies have found simple, practical ways to implement their programs and have achieved the benefits with little cost. The key factor in keeping the improvement effort simple is to start with documenting what is already in place in a way that all can share. From that point on, potential improvements can be identified, tried, installed and documented on a continuous basis. That approach is simple, is not costly and is good business.

> It is not enough to do your best; you must know what to do, and then do your best.
>
> W. Edwards Deming

Before

After

Where There's a Wall, There's a Way!
Achieving Group Consensus on What We Do

Introduction

When I was beginning to learn how to be a systems engineer, my mentor gave me some advice that has served me well. He told me, "Never try to solve a big problem on a small sheet of paper. Some problems just won't fit on 8.5 x 11." It turns out that this is true.

As an exercise in a class on project development life cycles, I asked everyone to draw a simple sketch – just five to seven blocks – indicating the major steps in their project life cycles, (e.g., a simple process flow chart). The results, as expected, were somewhat similar but there were significant differences among them. When we compared diagrams, we found different steps, different nomenclature and different understandings of the tasks involved in each of the blocks.

The class members were all from the same organization. The organization had a printed description of its approved standard life cycle and had mandated its use on all projects. In addition, all the participants in this class experienced the same training, which instructed them in the application and use of the standard life cycle.

So, how did this happen? Why was there so much variation in their exercise answers? As we discussed that question, several interesting points emerged.

Common Themes

First, and most amazing, was the fact that they all thought that they were following the standard. They all claimed to have planned their projects in accordance with their understanding of the standard and were executing in accordance with their project plan.

Several mentioned that they were concerned that other projects with which they interacted did not seem to be following the standard as closely as they were. Sometimes when they had finished the work in one phase of the cycle and were passing it on to the folks working on the next phase there were disagreements on the completeness or the contents of the deliverable. There were different perceptions of what should be done in each of the phases and what should be included in the products of the phase.

A third observation was that their upper management (in this case a group Director), never really got involved in developing or enforcing the standard process. The standard process was developed by the staff and issued over the signature of the senior manager at the time. However, the staff did not develop any reporting process to allow senior managers to check to see that projects were complying with the standard. The Director never saw the standard. It was signed and issued by his predecessor and he had no regular reporting that would even indicate that it existed. For him, the standard was totally invisible.

The class members described an essentially invisible standard. Sure, each step in the process was described in a book that everyone had on a shelf of standards documents. The standard steps were also described in a set of slides used in the training. But those slides were on the trainer's shelf.

The standard process was also in the minds of each of the project team members and managers as a mixture of their perceptions of the concepts and the details of what it was supposed to be. It was in each person's head but no one else could see it there. So, the standard process was invisible to all, not just the Director.

Agreeing on the Standard

I asked the class to speculate on how it might help if it were possible to get everyone to agree on the exact description of the standard life cycle and to operate in accordance with it. The class members suggested several benefits that might accrue. They suggested that having a clear, well understood path from start to finish should remove the current uncertainties about exactly what each team should be doing and when. Then, the team would become more confident that they were doing what they should be doing, not missing anything and not stepping on the toes of any of the other, related teams. Team members would know exactly what to do and could check off against the standard to know when they were done.

They thought it would eliminate the disagreements when going from one phase to the next. It would ensure that the work of each phase was complete and appropriate and ready to be used as the input to the next phase. One of the class members also observed that having a clear boundary would also prevent the team working on one phase from overshooting the boundary and attempting to do work that should be done in the next phase.

The last thing they mentioned was that if they were in full agreement and all saw the life cycle exactly the same it would be easy to check for compliance. There would be no opportunity for anyone to use the excuse, "I thought that was your responsibility."

We agreed on the potential benefits, but the class was skeptical. Short of having a mass meeting of all concerned, they thought that they could never get the kind of common understanding that would be required. One member mentioned the fact that there was regular, frequent turnover in the organization and within a few months you would have to have the same mass meeting again because 25 to 30 percent of the staff would have changed by then. In short, they didn't think it would be possible in their organization.

Going Public

I told them a true story about how another organization just like theirs had done it in a way that was ridiculously simple. Furthermore, it had worked and was continuing to work despite turnover in staff and management. It was done by creating and posting a big chart of the life cycle in a place where everyone would see it on a regular basis. They called the process "Going Public."

The organization was a 60-person contractor organization in Oak Ridge that was responding to government requests for changes to a large database. Over 50 such requests had to be handled each month. There was a company standard for handling change requests that included a detailed, step by step description of how it should be done. The manual was developed and issued by the corporate headquarters in Tysons Corner. All of the staff had been trained in the official life cycle.

However, the company books were on the shelves and the training was either forgotten or ignored. Each change request was handled individually in the way that the team leader felt would be best. Responsibilities for the individual steps in the process "happened" on an ad hoc basis. As you might expect, chaos reigned. There were always crises and misunderstandings of who should be doing what.

When we asked them about their process they said that it was written in the book, but they didn't follow it. We asked them to draw a picture of what they really did. They said they couldn't because everyone did his work differently. Just as we did in our class exercise, we asked them to each draw a high-level picture of their process for handling the requests. The results were the same as the results of the class exercise. When we compared them we found different steps, different nomenclature and different understandings of the tasks involved in each of the blocks. However, there was enough similarity that it appeared that the various approaches could be harmonized into a process that might work for everyone. They agreed to try to do that.

The way they approached it was interesting and effective. The leaders of the three teams worked together on a whiteboard to get agreement on the basic steps involved in the life cycle of a change. Then, they got a 15-foot long sheet of paper, laid out the basic process and posted the foundation diagram on the wall in a hallway that everyone passed through at least twice a day. They worked with each of the teams to fill in the details of each of the basic blocks. They put a box of sticky notes and some pens nearby and asked everyone to post comments and suggestions to improve how the chart illustrated exactly what they were doing.

Once a week the team leaders revisited and updated the chart to reflect the comments on the process trying to reconcile differences. Within a few weeks the comments converged, and an agreed process began to emerge. When we returned and asked to see their process, they pointed to their chart proudly and said, "This is it and we all are following it."

As evidence of that, they showed us their development folders. Each one had a list of the life cycle process steps printed on it and a place for initials to be applied as each step was completed and signed off by both the sender and the receiver. All the relevant documentation was recorded in each folder.

We then asked how it compared to the corporate standard. That sparked another review of their process relative to the corporate standard and major differences were discovered. At this point the team ownership of "their" life cycle was so strong that they agreed to recommend their process as a replacement for the corporate standard – and it was ultimately accepted.

Conclusion

The result of the process is that team members experienced the beneficial effects of having their own, visible life cycle almost immediately. There were fewer misunderstandings, fewer crises, team members could take vacations and someone could fill in for them because the work to be done at each stage was specified and would be done by a substitute just the same way that the original assignee would have done it. As turnover occurred, new team members were introduced to the chart and shown where they fit in the various processes. The chart was kept on the wall as a constant reference.

Some smiles began to appear on the faces of the team members. They told us, "It's really great to come to work and know exactly what I have to do today and when I've done it to be able to go home. No more crises and no more unscheduled overtime!" They proved the point that, **Where there's a wall, there's a way!**

My class members were impressed. They recognized that "Going Public" certainly had some possibility of helping them. We discussed whether the situation now was sufficiently painful for them that it would be worth the effort to replicate the work of the Oak Ridge team. Feelings were mixed, but some seemed to think it would be worth a try. All they had to do was go back to their office, gather their team, and find a wall.

=========================

Wish List

- ☐ No useless work
- ☐ No crises
- ☐ Realistic schedule
- ☐ No overloads
- ☐ Work- Life Balance
- ☐ Less overhead time
- ☐ Carefree vacations

Tangible Benefits of a Well-Defined Process

George Wonders Why

Our project team was together around the table at our weekly Brown Bag lunch. That's where we catch up with each other and share our ideas and concerns.

George, our team's work estimator and planner, brought up a subject that had been bothering him. He was upset by the new requirement from the corporate process improvement group. They are asking everyone to define and document the processes they follow. He complained that would be a lot of work. He said, "Look, I know what I do. Why should I have to write it down or draw a flowchart. I really don't see any benefit in doing it."

Genevieve and Ted responded. They had both previously worked at another company where the processes were well defined. They really liked the way things worked when their work was well defined. They both said that it was not only good for their company it was also good for them personally. They were eager to tell us about the benefits they got.

1. You Avoid Doing Useless Work

Genevieve asked us to think about the chaos on this project. Two people would sometimes be doing the same thing and they'd find out about it after they had spent time on it. Or, they would spend time on something early in the process that would be obsolete by the time it was really needed and would have to be redone.

In her earlier job, the processes were well defined and documented, Genevieve said. The process steps were all laid out and she could trust everyone else to do what they were supposed to do when they were supposed to do it.

When Genevieve and everyone else involved followed the process, she never found herself doing work that was not useful.

She could also look for and eliminate useless work. The bad stuff went away and nobody wasted time on it.

2. You Have Fewer (if any) Crises

Ted pointed out that when the process is not defined, you can never be sure that everything required has been done. He said that having a well-defined, documented process gets you a big bonus. You never get to **"Ooops! We forgot that task and have to work over the weekend to finish it!"** When the process is defined, and all the process steps are checked off, you don't have to waste time going back over things to see if the job is complete. You know that you are done. That kind of certainty is a blessing. You don't have to work late to catch up because of things being left undone.

3. Your Work Is Scheduled More Realistically

Ted continued, this time talking about the things that our scheduler, George, does. He said that, when there is no defined process, project estimators like you, may not be aware of some of the tasks involved and, as a result, they underbid the job. When the processes are not defined, every estimate is just a guess as to how much work is involved. That is, perhaps, the biggest cause of headaches for those of us who have to do the work. That is what turns our planned 40 hours of time into a 60+ hour work week. There's no joy in that.

Ted made another point. With good processes in place and being followed, estimators can see and estimate for all tasks involved in the job. Performance data on previous executions of the process can provide a sound basis of estimate for jobs that are similar to others. Estimates can be very accurate when all steps in a process are accounted for and comparable performance data can be found and used. When estimates are made this way, you can be confident that the estimated 40 hours of work will be done in 40 hours. No more uncompensated overtime. That's good for the estimator and good for the staff.

4. You Negotiate Your Schedule with Facts, Not Opinions

Genevieve then asked everyone to think about this situation. When you already have a lot of work to do and your boss asks you to take on some new, urgent task, you are defenseless if you don't have a defined process. You are in no position to describe what tasks you would have to put off in order to take on the new work. You sound really lame when all you can say is, "**Well, I'll have to put something else off to do that.**" And the boss says, "**What?**" – and you mumble your answer.

It's much better when you can take the boss to the process chart and the two of you can discuss, in detail, how much effort the new task will require and then see, specifically, what tasks will have to be put off to match the effort required for the new work.

5. You Get Your Non-Work Life Back

As lunch ended we listed the benefits we had talked about:

- You know what you have to do, and you know when you're done
- You avoid useless work
- Crises and your extra work to make up for them are eliminated
- No uncompensated overtime is needed to make up for underestimates
- You avoid the anguish of having to handle "urgent" along with regular work
- Easier training means that bringing new people on board doesn't detract from your productive time

Even George agreed that such savings could end our 60+ hour weeks. We might also find that we would have a couple of hours to think about how to improve what we do.

6. You Spend Less Time Training

Sally then spoke up. She said that she had read in Fred Brooks' book, '***The Mythical Man-Month',*** that adding people to a project running late will slow it down and make it even later. Why? Because the staff members who were already working hard to meet the deadline would have to take time to train the reinforcements in the process. She thought that having a defined process would make training easier and would help when we had to bring in extra help to recover from a slippage or handle an overload. She thought, and everyone agreed, that it would be better when you have a picture of your process you can show to the reinforcements. Then, instead of having to describe each step you would just have to be available for questions.

7. Bonus Benefit

Before we broke up, Genevieve and Ted said that there was one benefit we had not talked about but, it really meant a lot to them personally. That was the fact that they could now take their planned vacations whenever they wanted and would not have to worry about getting an urgent call about something that was supposed to be being handled by someone back at the office. In their prior organization, with defined processes in place, it was clear what had to be done and no calls were required. So, Genevieve and Ted added "***Peace of Mind While on Vacation***" to the list.

As we left, Ted said that he hoped we would get our processes defined and documented soon. He assured us that it would be worth the effort – that we would save time, be more productive, and would find work more enjoyable. He has worked that way, he should know.

George was willing to give it a try.

Do-It-Yourself

A task checklist is the simplest way to define your process and incorporate some of the benefits of this idea.

Another common approach is to define processes in a procedures document. Have you ever drawn a picture of your process to see if the words are telling the right story — what you really do?

To read more about how to start obtaining these benefits, see Bill's book, Draw What You Do. Amazon.com, 2013

==

Wish List
Accomplished
- ✓ No useless work
- ✓ No crises
- ✓ Realistic schedule
- ✓ No overloads
- ✓ Work- Life Balance
- ✓ Less overhead time
- ✓ Carefree vacations

The Project Manager's Mirror

In the Store

At a local Pawn shop I saw something that was labeled "Project Manager's Mirror." The manager said that it was quite old and had some remarkable powers. First, it could talk. Second, it always told the truth. This sounded interesting and the shop owner wasn't asking much, so I bought it and took it home and hung it on the wall.

The next day, I looked into the mirror and it spoke. It asked me:

"How are your projects going?"

I said, "We're doing just fine."

The mirror replied: *"No you're not! ...and here's why. [The mirror spoke in bullet points]*

- *Your team members make lots of mistakes*
- *Some of your products get rejected*
- *You sometimes waste time with duplicate or unnecessary work*
- *You fall behind on schedules and don't know how much work is still left to be done to catch up*
- *You go on vacation and have to come back because of a crisis*

...and there's lots more... How can you say you are 'Doing fine'?"

I told the mirror that those things were just the normal things that always happen and they were not really a problem. The mirror almost jumped off the wall with its answer. It said:

"You say it's not a problem!!!!! You've got to be kidding. You have competition that is more efficient than you. Your customer really cares about how long it takes you to get things done or get them done right and could drop you at any time for someone better.

> *Your team members care about working nights and weekends on unscheduled overtime. Don't you see that?"*

I answered by telling the mirror that it is sort of inevitable that those kinds of things happen. Every job is different. The mirror replied:

> *"You know that every job is different, so why don't you have a process that deals effectively with that situation? Auto repair shops do that – the better shops are set up to be prepared to deal quickly and efficiently with all the various things that go wrong with cars. You should be adjusting your processes so you can handle all the variations in your projects."*

This was getting a bit annoying, so I decided to give the mirror a little dose of reality. I said, "Look, there's nothing I can do. The company staff guys talk like you. They keep saying that I need to set up a process improvement system. I'd do that, but it would take a lot of effort and we don't have any to spare."

Once more the mirror spoke:

> *"Please remember, I always tell the truth. Setting up to do continuous process improvement does not take long and does not cost a lot. You can do it just like a little project.*
>
> *You already have a process. It's what you are doing now. You can start by looking at a part of it where some of your problems come from. If you have been missing some schedules, take a look at how you go about estimating time and effort. You could draw a flowchart of how you do that. Then, you and your team can all look at it together and see where you can make some improvements and start doing it the better way.*
>
> *After you've done that, pick another target and do the same."*

I told the mirror: "We are already working 50-60-hour weeks. We don't have any time to do this kind of thing."

> *"If you thought this was important you could find time to do this. This is the kind of thing that you can all do at your brown bag lunches. You can skip some of the sports talk and instead talk about what you do and how you can do it better. Lots of people do it this way.*

> *Most of my previous owners said that it took them less than two hours a week to get things going and within six months they were saving more time than that – and I agreed with them."*

"Ok Mirror, I'll get right on it today."

> "Sure, you will – and pigs will start flying tomorrow. Today will be just like yesterday. You'll go in to work and the first little thing that comes up will grab your attention and you'll forget all about what we've been talking about – doing fire prevention rather than just fighting fires. And tomorrow will be the same and you will keep saying, 'I'll get right on it.'"

I got really annoyed at that and decided to hit back. "Look here, Mirror. If you're so smart, how come I found you in a pawn shop? Your last owner must have wanted to get rid of you."

> *"My last owner was different from all of those before him. He didn't listen to me and didn't do what I said.*
>
> *Instead of fixing his processes he kept trying to fix his problems one at a time. He got worn out. His company failed. He lost his job. He needed money, so he brought me here.*

> *Please don't be like him. It's lonely in the Pawn Shop."*

===

The Rule of Fred

When things go poorly, a team will easily break up and everyone will point fingers. Who's to blame?

"The team is very disappointed Fred at your failure!"

If a team doesn't have a Fred, they should get one, in case there's a failure! It's much easier to blame Fred than to take responsibility as a team.

When Fred succeeds, the team succeeds and can cheer its success as a team. But when Fred fails, the team can scorn him and boo him and tell him, to work harder, or smarter or something.

"If only Fred had been a team player, we would have succeeded!"

This is the Rule of Fred.

Jason Giecek

REPEALED

Repealing the Rule of Fred

Now that you have read the stories, you can see why we should never blame Fred or Freda. The problem is always **the process.**

Some Examples

Something has gone wrong on your team's project. Your schedule has started to slip, the new product you are all working on is not working right, and the project is starting to go over budget or --- something else.

> *"The process is taking too much time to complete his tasks."*
>
> *"The process is overrunning his budget."*
>
> *"The process is using the wrong materials."*
>
> *"The process forgot to include the critical part."*
>
> *... and so on.*

How did those things happen?

- The process wasn't clear.
- The process did not call for the right tools and materials
- The process did not include proper training for the staff
- The process did not properly align inputs and outputs for the various tasks
- The process did not allow enough time to do the work properly

It's All About Process

There are some fortunate souls who work where the work processes are well-defined and maintained and work always goes smoothly. However, there are still many places where problems like those mentioned above continue to occur frequently and the teams just continue to blame someone and never look for the real cause of the problems. So, the local "Freds" or "Fredas" keep getting blamed, the faulty processes remain unchanged, and the problems continue. That's no fun for anyone.

How to Repeal the Rule of Fred

When you start to see symptoms of process problems, here are some things you need to do.

First, get with your co-workers and discuss what you are doing and discuss what you are doing and how you are going about it. Sharing what you all know about how your processes work is the key. Even in the most dedicated and cohesive work groups there can be significant differences in understanding "how we do things." You must work together to discover how your processes work. Here are some steps you can take to aid in the sharing.

- ☐ Identify the processes critical to your success
- ☐ Display your processes so you can all see and agree on how they must work
- ☐ Find and fix process steps that cause problems
- ☐ Document your results
- ☐ Make this type of sharing continuous.

Remember: Fix the process – Don't blame Fred.

Fred in a Blame-Free environment.

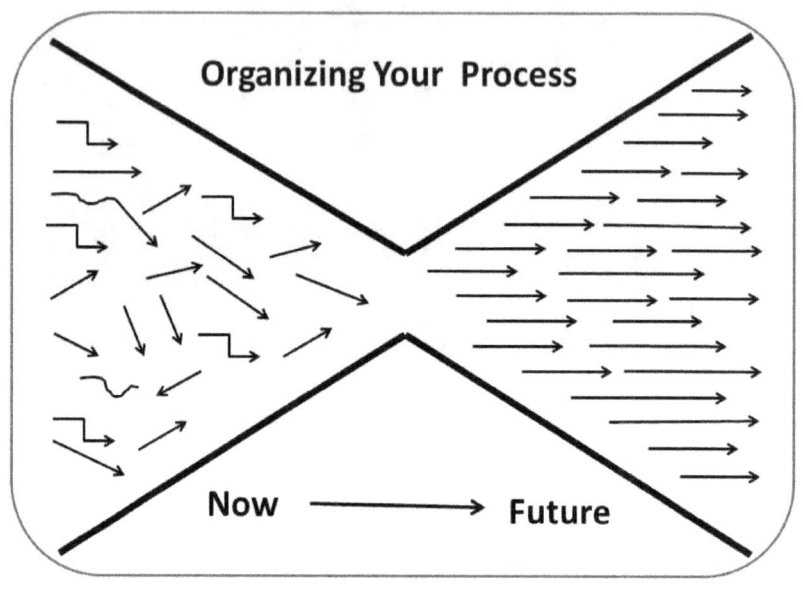

Process Definition Practice Exercise

Do you have any of these problems?

- Some confusion about who does what
- "Bad" surprises and crises
- Too many late nights
- Faulty products that get out the door
- Late deliveries

These are all symptoms of problems somewhere in your processes. In order to fix these, you and your co-workers all have to be able to see where they are occurring and then agree on the best way to fix them.

Getting to where you can all share what you know about how your processes work is the key. Even in the most dedicated and cohesive work groups there can be significant differences in understanding "how we do things". You need work together to discover your processes.

Here is a two-part exercise that will give you a start.

Typical Morning Routine Tasks List

- Get Up
- Make your bed
- Use bathroom
- Turn on TV for News or Weather
- Choose clothes
- Exercise
- Dress
- Make coffee
- Make breakfast
- Eat Breakfast
- Make and pack lunch
- Do Housework
- Read paper
- Check traffic reports
- Load briefcase/backpack
- Dress for weather
- Check e-mail, Smart Phone for messages
- Leave house
- Go back for something you forgot

Process Definition Exercise # 1 – Part 1 of 2

Getting Up and Out - Part 1

Objective: To provide experience in defining a process, (i.e., Drawing What You Do)

Scenario

Your process for getting up and going to work includes activities involving: dressing; morning ablutions; communications (tv/phone/computer); food and beverage; and any other relevant activities. You have probably set up a fairly routine process for doing this. This exercise will give you an opportunity to define and document that process so that you can discuss it with others.

Tasks

Develop a flow chart for the "standard" process you go through from the time you get up until you leave the house to go to school or work. A list of typical tasks is on Page 68

If there are variations in the process by day of the week or other factors note them separately.

Limit your list of tasks to no more than 20 items.

Note typical start and end times for the process.

Timing

Allow 15-20 minutes for this exercise.

Results Expected

- A flow chart of your standard routine
- You should be prepared to present your chart and discuss:
    - Any difficulties you experienced in developing the chart
    - Any insights you gained from this exercise
- Save your work for later use in Part 2

Typical Morning Routine Tasks List

(This time, for <u>three people</u> sharing the same house)

- Get Up
- Make your bed
- Use bathroom
- Turn on TV for News or Weather
- Choose clothes
- Dress
- Make coffee
- Make breakfast
- Eat Breakfast
- Make and pack lunch
- Check traffic reports
- Load briefcase/backpack
- Dress for weather
- Check e-mail, Smart Phone for messages
- Leave house
- Go back for something you forgot
- Walk/drive/bus
- Whatever …

Process Definition Exercise # 2– Part 2 of 2

Getting Up and Out - Part 2

Objective: To provide experience in "Drawing What You Do" **when you are doing it with others.**

Scenario

You each have defined and documented a fairly routine process for getting up and going to work.

In Part 1, we found out that most people include the same steps for this process, however, there are some significant variations among them in the sequence in which they perform those tasks. This exercise will give you an opportunity to practice resolving the differences.

For this exercise we will assume that you have two visitors come to stay with you for a few weeks and you need to modify your process to accommodate their needs as well as your own.

Tasks

- Share the flow charts you and your visitors developed in Part 1.
- Discuss the differences
- Develop a flow chart for a process that will accommodate everyone in an acceptable way.

Timing

Work in teams of three for this exercise. Allow 20-30 minutes.

Results Expected

- A flow chart of your agreed routine
- You should be prepared to present your chart and discuss:
    - Any difficulties you experienced in developing the chart
    - Any insights you gained from this exercise
- Save your work for later use in case you have visitors.

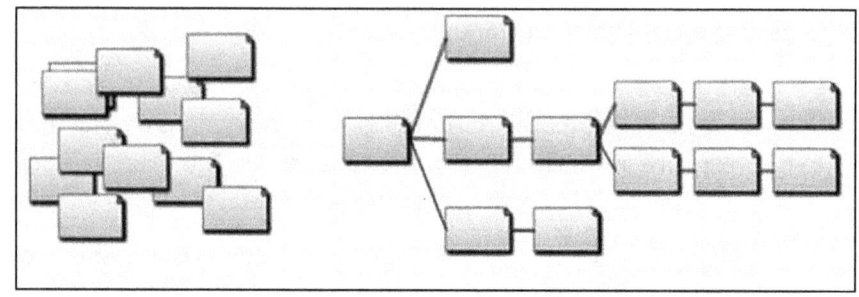

Exercise Follow-Up

To Do List

1. Work with your staff to draw a picture of your process (what you do now and how you do it)
2. Look for things you could do better and change the picture to match
3. Start following the process you all agreed on
4. Measure to see what works well and what needs to be changed
5. Change the process to improve performance
6. Keep track of the performance improvements and make them known
7. Remember --- **It's always the <u>process</u>!**

Other Books by Bill Flury

Draw What You Do: A Practical Approach to Process Improvement
    ISBN-13: 9781494275181
    ISBN-10: 149427518X

WYSIWYG Tales: See and Improve What You Do
    ISBN-13: 978-1494256975
    ISBN-10: 1494256975

A Tinkerer's Notebook: Sharing the Joy of Tinkering
    ISBN-13: 978-1539788508
    ISBN-10: 1539788504

www.ingramcontent.com/pod-product-compliance
Lightning Source LLC
Chambersburg PA
CBHW070316230526
45470CB00002B/903